YOU CHOOSE

CAN YOU ESCAPE
A HAUNTED
HOSPITAL?

An Interactive
Paranormal Adventure

by Ailynn Collins

Published by Capstone Press, an imprint of Capstone
1710 Roe Crest Drive, North Mankato, Minnesota 56003
capstonepub.com

Copyright © 2026 by Capstone. All rights reserved. No part of this publication may be reproduced in whole or in part, or stored in a retrieval system, or transmitted in any form or by any means, electronic, mechanical, photocopying, recording, or otherwise, without written permission of the publisher.

Library of Congress Cataloging-in-Publication Data is available
on the Library of Congress website.
ISBN: 9798875210198 (hardcover)
ISBN: 9798875210167 (paperback)
ISBN: 9798875210174 (ebook PDF)

Summary: Readers explore haunted hospitals around the world and experience paranormal activity that has been inspired by reports from real people.

Editorial Credits
Editor: Carrie Sheely; Designer: Elijah Blue; Media Researcher: Rebekah Hubstenberger; Production Specialist: Tori Abraham

Photo Credits
Alamy: Sarah Thornton, 102, This Old Postcard, 72; Associated Press: David Smith, 107; Getty Images: Cavan Images, 100, DrPixel, 92, Freaktography Photography, 83, iStock/Davide Zanin, 53, iStock/Ivan Zastavetskyi, 32, iStock/Kai Malte, 16, iStock/sivarock, 40, iStock/Vladimir Zapletin, 63, Maximilian Mueller, 55, Stefan Baumann, 86; Shutterstock: Chadchai Krisadapong, 60, emma.candid, 39, Juiced Up Media, 21, 105, Kirk Fisher, 10, Milosz Maslanka, 27, Mo Photography Berlin, 47, Stephan Bezuidenhout, 6, Vladimir Mulder, cover

Design Elements
Capstone: Dina Her; Shutterstock: Nik Merkulov, Olha Nion

Any additional websites and resources referenced in this book are not maintained, authorized, or sponsored by Capstone. All product and company names are trademarks™ or registered® trademarks of their respective holders.

Printed and bound in China. 006276

TABLE OF CONTENTS

INTRODUCTION
About Your Adventure............5

CHAPTER 1
Spine-Tingling Vacation Spots......7

CHAPTER 2
St. Ignatius Hospital............11

CHAPTER 3
Old Changi Hospital............41

CHAPTER 4
Tranquille Sanatorium..........73

CHAPTER 5
Haunted Hospitals............103

More Ghostly Encounters........106
Other Paths to Explore..........108
Glossary.....................109
Select Bibliography.............110
Read More...................111
Internet Sites.................111
About the Author..............112

INTRODUCTION
ABOUT YOUR ADVENTURE

YOU are about to explore three run-down abandoned hospitals. What can be found there? Not just rubble, dust, and items left behind. These hospitals are said to be some of the most haunted in the world! Can you escape a haunted hospital?

Chapter One sets the scene. Then you choose which path to read. Follow the directions at the bottom of the page. Your decisions will change your outcome. After you finish one path, go back and read the others for new perspectives and more adventures.

Turn the page to begin your adventure.

CHAPTER 1
SPINE-TINGLING VACATION SPOTS

At breakfast this morning, your parents announced that you get to pick the next vacation destination.

"Me?" you squeal. "Do you mean I can pick anywhere, and you'll go?"

Dad shakes his head while sipping his coffee. "Within reason, of course."

Turn the page.

You jump up from the table and run to grab a book you've just checked out from the library. It's about haunted hospitals. You love scary things and places. While reading, you were wishing you could visit these places. Now's your chance. You can't wait to show your parents the book.

"Look at this," you say, opening the book in the middle of the table. "There's a haunted hospital that will take only about three hours to travel to in a car. There are also some in other countries. They're all great places for vacation with the added treat of a scary experience. Wouldn't you love to meet ghosts from all over? Please, can we pick one of these places?"

Your parents look over your suggestions. They agree that each place has some great vacation experiences.

"But are you sure you want to be scared on vacation?" Mom asks, looking worried.

"Yes!" you say. You've been reading about haunted places for so long. You can't wait to experience one for real. "It'll be fun."

"Be careful what you wish for," Dad says. "Meeting a ghost may be a lot scarier than you expect."

You're so happy to hear his warning. You spend all day thinking about where you'd like to go.

Which hospital will you visit?

- To visit St. Ignatius Hospital in Colfax, Washington, turn to page 11.
- To visit the Old Changi Hospital in Changi, Singapore, turn to page 41.
- To visit the Tranquille Sanatorium in Kamloops, Canada, turn to page 73.

CHAPTER 2
ST. IGNATIUS HOSPITAL

You step out of the car at St. Ignatius Hospital as the sun begins to set.

"Are you ready for this?" Dad asks, grinning.

"Of course I am!" you say.

A young man with a thick beard appears from the front door of the red brick hospital. "Welcome to the ghost tour," he says loudly. You, your parents, and ten other people gather around him. "My name is Tom, and I'm a ghost hunter. I'll be your guide tonight."

Turn the page.

He begins with a history of the place. "The hospital opened in 1893. It stayed in business until 1964 as a hospital. Then it was used as a mental health facility and an assisted living home. It closed its doors in 2003 and was abandoned for many years. It was bought by Austin and Laura Storm in 2021. They've been restoring the historical site. They opened it up for visitors to help raise money for the restoration."

"It doesn't sound like a terribly scary place," Mom remarks.

Tom continues. "The first death here was recorded in June 1893. It was a man named F. E. Martin. He was a railroad worker who was crushed between railcars. His ghost is said to still haunt the hospital hallways. People say they've encountered other spirits here too."

"Well, that sounds pretty scary!" you say.

Tom ushers everyone into the building. The small lobby is clean but in need of some work. The paint on the walls is peeling, and there's debris everywhere.

Tom shows you a table that has pieces of equipment laid out on it.

"These are some of the things ghost hunters use," he says. "These full-spectrum cameras can see more than a regular camera. They work well in the dark and pick up small differences in light and shadow." He demonstrates how to use them.

He picks up something that looks like a TV remote control. "This is an EMF reader. It picks up changes in the electromagnetic field. When you enter a room, these lights may flash, telling you that something supernatural could be present."

Turn the page.

Tom offers these and flashlights to everyone on the tour. "Take what you're comfortable with," he says. "You never know what you might come across."

You pick up the EMF reader. Your parents play with a video camera.

"If there's a lot of paranormal activity tonight, we may only be able to visit a part of the hospital," Tom announces. "Among the wards upstairs is one of the most well-known rooms. It belonged to a patient named Rose. We could start there, or we could explore the first floor where many experiences have been reported."

- To see the wards upstairs, go to page 15.
- To tour the first floor, turn to page 20.

You decide that going upstairs is a safer choice.

You follow Tom as he climbs the stairs. As you walk through the door at the landing, the yellow light on your EMF reader flickers uncertainly.

"That's strange," you say to yourself. "This building has no electricity. This shouldn't happen."

Tom leads your group through several large areas. "These were the old hospital rooms," he explains as he moves through quickly.

He pauses in a smaller room with an enclosed porch. It has windows on three sides.

"What was this room used for?" you ask, noticing that a window on the side is broken.

Turn the page.

"This is where patients sat to get some sunshine while being isolated from others," Tom explains. He gestures to the window that overlooks a garden below. "The hospital treated people with a disease called tuberculosis. They had to be kept apart from others to help keep it from spreading."

You peek through a smaller broken window to the side and see a room with an attached toilet area. You'd hate to be a patient here and have people watch you use the toilet.

You turn to tell Mom, but her face has gone white. She's staring into the room behind you.

You follow her gaze and see something grayish that could be the outline of a person, but it's blurry. When you shine your light into the room, the figure disappears. It must be a trick of the lighting. "Are you okay, Mom?" you whisper.

Before she can answer, Tom speaks. "We can move on to our most famous room. Or we could head to the upper floor."

Mom's face is still pale. "I think I'd rather see the upper floors," she says.

You want to be considerate of her feelings, but Rose's room was the place you wanted to see most.

- To go to the upper floors, turn to page 18.
- To go to Rose's room, turn to page 24.

That blurry outline scared you a bit too, so you choose to go upstairs.

Some in the group insist on going to Rose's room. Tom tells them they can take a quick peek and meet the rest of the group afterward.

"That's the most well-known room in the hospital," Dad says. "I won't be long." He heads off to Rose's room with several others.

You follow Tom and Mom to the top floor instead. It's much neater up here. Most of the debris has been cleared away.

You walk in silence from room to room. Tom takes some photos with a camera. But when you look at the screen, the photos don't show anything unusual. Your EMF reader blinks occasionally, but not for long enough to mean anything.

"Try this room," Tom suggests.

You push your reader out into the room Tom indicates. The lights on your reader stay on longer than before. Tom snaps a few photos. His camera screen shows a shadow at the end of the room. It's roughly in the shape of a person.

"Maybe we want to find a ghost so badly, we'd see it in anything," you say, doubtfully.

Tom smiles. "Should we summon a ghost?" he asks. "It's worked for me before."

You look to Mom. She's unsure but says nothing.

- To summon a ghost, turn to page 27.
- To keep exploring this floor, turn to page 30.

"I vote to explore this floor first," you say.

"Let's head to the kitchen then," Tom says, taking you all down a long hallway.

You enter a large room that smells damp and musty. The walls are crumbling and there's debris on the floor. There's a wide, rusty stove along one broken wall. Cabinets line the other walls. Their doors hang loosely on their hinges.

"I'm going to summon a ghost," Tom continues. "There was a patient here named Rose. Today happens to be her birthday. Perhaps she'll make her presence known. Shall we try?"

People murmur uncertainly.

Tom begins. "Rose, are you here? We'd like to wish you a happy birthday."

Your parents start their video camera. Others click away, hoping to capture something. You look down at your EMF reader. A yellow light goes on and then off.

Tom sees it and continues. "Rose, are you here?"

The yellow light comes on again. Then the green and red lights flash. Each bulb blinks in a dance of twinkling lights.

EMF reader

Turn the page.

"Thank you for gracing us with your presence," Tom says, excitedly.

"I think we captured something," Mom's voice echoes off the walls. You gather around her small video screen on the camera.

It shows a dark kitchen. But there's a fuzzy figure, like a cloud of smoke, right by the stove. It could be a person. Or it could be your imagination.

"Happy birthday, Rose," you say.

Several minutes pass. No one hears or sees anything more. The instruments are all silent.

Tom shrugs. "I guess she's not very communicative today," he says. "Let's leave her and move on."

Disappointed, you linger a little longer in the kitchen as the others file out. Then you hear knocking noises. It sounds like someone is knocking on the walls. The sounds stop just as suddenly as they started.

Tom appears at the doorway. "Are you coming?"

You hurry out of the kitchen to join your parents. You try to convince yourself that the sounds were your imagination.

Tom moves to the front of the group. "When this building was a hospital, the morgue was in the basement. Shall we go there?" he asks. "If not, we could walk through the wards. There might be a surprisingly spooky room. Where would you like to go?"

- To go to the morgue, turn to page 33.
- To walk through the wards, turn to page 37.

Mom sees that you really want to go to Rose's room. "I'll wait downstairs for you," she offers.

Tom leads the group down a narrow hallway. Debris lies all over the floor, so you step carefully. As you walk, you hear someone sighing. Dad hears it too. You cling to him tightly.

"I don't think I'm as brave as I thought I was," you whisper as you reach the end of the hallway.

The group stops outside the last room. It's dimly lit. You get an uneasy feeling.

Tom allows people in two at a time. You and Dad are last in line.

The room is small with a rusty metal bed frame in a corner. Next to it is a small heater and an old TV.

Someone has splattered red paint on the wall to make it look like blood. Creepy!

"According to the stories, Rose was a very troubled patient," Tom says. "She screamed a lot. This disturbed other patients, so the hospital made this room soundproof."

You shiver at the thought of Rose screaming. You feel sorry that she struggled so much.

"She lived here till she died, and her spirit still haunts the room," Tom says.

The room gives you chills. Dad films with his video camera as you put a hand on the head of the metal bed frame. It's icy cold.

"There's nothing unusual here," Dad says, putting down his camera. He leaves the room. You follow, heading toward the door.

Turn the page.

That's when you hear a buzzing sound. Turning back, you see that it's the TV.

A face appears on the screen. It's a girl with disheveled hair. She mouths, *Go away!*

Tom appears next to you. "That's never happened before," he gasps. You both bolt down the stairs.

Mom is waiting for you in the front lobby. She follows you as you run out into the night air.

Dad emerges from the building. He looks pretty pale too.

"I've had enough," you say. "Let's go home."

Your parents don't argue. You don't even tell Tom you're leaving.

THE END

To follow another path, turn to page 11.
To learn more about haunted hospitals, turn to page 103.

"Let's do it!" you say, shivering. Is it excitement or fear?

Tom picks a room. "This is what we call the children's room," he says. He points out the games and toys that previous ghost hunters have left for the ghosts here. "These spirits have been the least angry. Let's see if anyone is here."

Turn the page.

Tom begins to call out to the spirits. "Is anyone here tonight? Would you like to play a game?"

You stare at a board game by the window. "I think that piece just moved!" you gasp.

"I saw that too!" Mom agrees.

"Thank you," Tom says, enthusiastically. "If you're doing well tonight and would like us to stay, please move the green game piece. If you'd like to be left alone, move the red one."

None of you move or breathe. You wait for what feels like an eternity. Then the red piece on the game board topples over.

You exhale. "We'll leave you alone," you say. "We're sorry we bothered you."

Tom looks disappointed. He leads you back downstairs. You meet up with the rest of the group. Most of them look pale and terrified.

Nobody discusses what they've experienced until you're all outside the hospital.

"What a night," Dad says. "I've had quite enough."

"Me too!" you and Mom say at the same time.

You head to your hotel.

"That was scary, but I'm glad we did it," you say. "Now I can say that I've encountered an actual ghost."

Mom and Dad shrug. They don't say much about the experience.

THE END

To follow another path, turn to page 11.
To learn more about haunted hospitals, turn to page 103.

"No, thank you," you say, a little disappointed. You want to be considerate of Mom's feelings.

Mom clings to you as you walk through the rest of the rooms. At some points, you think you hear whispers, but neither of you can agree on that. She hears stuff you don't, and you hear stuff she doesn't. So, can it be real?

You walk the entire floor. Nothing extraordinary happens. Finally, you make your way back down to the ground floor. You meet Dad and the other people in your group. They have found nothing.

"I enjoyed the history of the place," Dad says, looking through the video he's taken. "Pity the ghosts were all asleep tonight." He laughs at his own silly joke.

Your group gathers at the entrance.

"I know we didn't see or hear any ghosts tonight, but I hope you all had a good time," Tom says.

Everyone says yes. You think about the shadow you and Mom saw on the video camera screen and wonder if you should say something. You decide to stay quiet.

As your car pulls away from the hospital, you look back at the building. Someone is standing at a window on the top floor.

"Stop!" you call out without thinking.

Dad stops the car, and you all look back. In the moonlight, you can see a woman in a white gown with long hair that shields her features.

"Do you think someone is still in the building?" Mom asks.

Turn the page.

Neither you nor Dad answers. You all know that Tom locked up when you left him. So who is the woman in the window?

THE END

To follow another path, turn to page 11.
To learn more about haunted hospitals, turn to page 103.

"Let's go to the morgue!" you say. That's where all the action happens.

The group descends the stairs in silence. Mom squeezes your hand.

At the bottom of the stairs, it's dark. Flashlights click on. The beams of light cast shadows everywhere. Tom leads you to the very end of the hallway.

"This room has been reported to have many paranormal sightings," Tom says in a low voice.

Tom asks you all to stand in a circle. "Those of you with EMF readers, place them in front of you so we can all see," he instructs. "Those with cameras, get ready to capture photos and video."

You brace yourself.

Turn the page.

"Who is here tonight?" Tom asks, closing his eyes. "Fred, Sister Johanna, Lily?"

It seems to you that Tom is just listing a bunch of names. Does he really know the names of the people who died here?

"Fred, are you here tonight?" Tom tries again.

Mom gasps. She's staring at the reader in your hand. Its lights are blinking!

Other readers begin to light up as well. Those with video cameras begin to film.

"Fred!" Tom opens his eyes. "Thank you for joining us tonight." He grins as he looks around at the group. Most people are shocked. Some are skeptical. You aren't quite sure what to feel. Tom could be saying a ghost is here just to entertain the group.

The flashlights cast strange shadows against the walls. Tom takes a photo with his full-spectrum camera and examines the result on the little screen.

"Look at this," he says, delighted. "He really is here."

The screen shows a picture of colors—mostly green along the sides and floor of the room. But by the window at the end, there's a blob of pinkish red. Could that be Fred?

"What if it's not Fred?" you ask.

"Well, let's find out," Tom replies. "Are you another patient?" he asks.

All the EMF readers light up with green lights. That means yes.

"Ouch!" someone in the group cries out.

Turn the page.

One by one, everyone in the group feels something slap them. You feel it at the back of your head. Everyone rushes out of the morgue. Clearly this ghost is upset at your presence.

You reach the front garden quickly. The fresh air feels good. Everyone in the group discusses what happened in low voices. You're all shaken by the experience.

When Tom asks if anyone would like to head back inside, no one answers. You spend the rest of the tour walking the grounds outside instead. You've all had enough of the supernatural for tonight.

THE END

To follow another path, turn to page 11.
To learn more about haunted hospitals, turn to page 103.

"It would be great to see the wards to learn how patients lived in this hospital," you say.

No one objects. Tom leads you all down another hallway. You walk into a narrow room with damaged cupboards lining both walls.

This room has to be worse than a morgue! The cupboards are filled with old dolls. They sit or stand along the broken cabinet doors. Their faces are streaked with dirt, and their hair is messy. Some look like they've been in a fight!

Suddenly, Tom begins to laugh, low and slow. This is an eerie sound.

"Please don't do that," you tell him. The sound makes you sick to your stomach.

Turn the page.

Tom keeps making the deep chuckling sound. Others repeat your request, but he doesn't stop. Finally, Dad grabs Tom by the arms and shakes him gently. This brings Tom's attention back to the group.

"What were you saying?" he asks, as if he'd been in conversation with your dad.

"You were laughing," Dad says. "It was creepy."

Tom looks puzzled. "Are you sure? I don't remember that."

"Okay," you say, raising both hands in surrender. "I'm out of here. This is way too spooky for me." You hurry out of the room.

You glance over at the dolls once more. One of them is bald with only one eye. It winks at you. You get out of there fast.

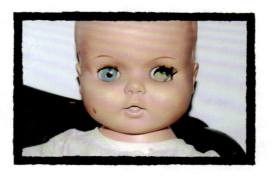

You grab Mom's hand and pull her back down the stairs and out the front door.

"That was a fun evening," Mom says as you both step out into the cool night air. You can tell from her shaky voice that she doesn't really mean it.

You breathe a sigh of relief. This hospital has certainly lived up to its reputation as being one of the most haunted places in the country. You're glad you made it out safely.

THE END

To follow another path, turn to page 11.
To learn more about haunted hospitals, turn to page 103.

CHAPTER 3
OLD CHANGI HOSPITAL

You've arrived at the island nation of Singapore. It's filled with tall buildings and busy streets. But you're especially interested in a haunted hospital called the Old Changi. You're very lucky to have gotten the last three spots on the hospital tour.

The sun is just setting as a taxi drops you off at Old Changi Hospital. You walk through the gate and take in the large white buildings. One building has open walkways on either side of the middle section. Another building, with "Changi Hospital" on the side, is several stories high with lots of windows.

Turn the page.

You meet the guides, Mat and Farah, and join a group of 17 other tourists. Mat gathers the group on the patch of grass in front of the hospital.

"Welcome," he begins. "Farah and I will be taking you around the grounds tonight."

Farah points to the hilltop building partially hidden behind some trees. "These buildings were built between 1935 and 1962 by the British when they ruled Singapore. We gained independence in 1965."

You follow Mat and Farah up through the door of the original hospital.

"This building was used as military barracks and as a hospital at different times," Farah says.

The group moves into one of the large rooms. The walls are covered in graffiti and the paint is peeling.

"The British housed thousands of soldiers here before World War II," Mat says. "When the Japanese invaded Singapore, they used it as a hospital for their wounded soldiers. The other buildings held prisoners of war."

You wander out to the hallway and lean over the balcony to catch a breeze. You notice a figure standing in a window in the building across the way. He's dressed in a loose white shirt and baggy pants. It must be another tourist. You watch him as he disappears into a room.

Turn the page.

When you turn back, you realize you're all alone. The group has moved on without you. You're annoyed your parents didn't wait for you.

You hear voices and follow the sound. With each step, everything around you grows darker. The sun has finally set.

"Hello?" you call out. "Where did everyone go?"

No one answers, but you can hear voices coming from the left. Then you catch a glimpse of a group of people disappearing into a room on the right.

You're confused. Should you follow the people into the room or follow the voices?

- To follow the people, go to page 45.
- To follow the voices, turn to page 48.

You trust your eyes more than your ears, so you head to the right. As you enter one room, the group disappears into another. No matter how fast you move, the group seems to stay one step ahead of you.

Your frustration grows. It feels like one of those dreams where you can't reach the place you're trying to get to, no matter how hard you try.

You follow the group up a back staircase. When you get to the top, you're winded. You sit down on a step. Whispers are coming from somewhere above. But it's not in English. You get up and follow the sound anyway. It takes you to the top floor. It's a mess here. Tiles have been dug up, and the floor is uneven. You step carefully.

Turn the page.

The whispers grow louder, and you cut through a smaller open area to another ward-like room. Your toe catches on some debris, and you fall.

"Ouch!" you say as you land on your knees. Examining the skin there, you see blood.

"Help!" you call out, hoping that your tour group is somewhere on this floor.

A woman appears rather suddenly in front of you. She's dressed in what looks like a nurse uniform. Maybe she's the first aid person for the tour or a paid actor to be in character. You don't really care. You tell her what's happened.

"Are you able to walk?" she asks. "We have a first aid room in the other building where the emergency department is."

You wonder if she misspoke. Surely, the emergency department used to be there and is now only a first aid station for tourists and visitors.

"I can walk," you say. "But could you find my parents, please?" Mom always has a first aid kit in her bag. You'd prefer that she takes care of you.

The woman purses her lips. "Just come with me," she insists.

- To wait for Mom, turn to page 54.
- To go with the nurse, turn to page 57.

You follow the voices. Climbing steep steps, you find that everyone is outside in an open area.

You're relieved to catch up with your parents. They smile at you as if they didn't notice you were gone. Farah's telling everyone about this place.

"This was the main administration building," she says. "It was also a casualty entrance."

You walk through the courtyard. There are pillars lining the open hallway.

Farah points to rooms along the front of the building. "These were operating theaters," she says.

She leads the group up a ramp past the first-floor rooms. You walk in silence.

"This is one linkway between this building and the newer block," Farah explains. "It was built in 1962 and was a great relief to everyone. Before this, they had to climb more than 80 steps to get to the higher building." She laughs.

"When the Japanese imprisoned enemy soldiers here, it's said that terrible things were done to them," Mat adds. "We don't like to talk about it, but this area gives me chills."

Several people shiver visibly. Mom grabs onto Dad's arm. You try not to look into the dark rooms.

Farah leads you into a large room with wooden slats on the windows. Lighting on the floor casts an eerie glow. On the floor in the middle of the room, someone has drawn a pentacle. You have read it can be a symbol of witchcraft.

Turn the page.

Farah explains that people like to sneak into these buildings to try to find ghosts and communicate with the spirits.

"Nothing unusual has been proven," she says. "But the internet is full of stories of the paranormal found here."

You notice that people walk around the drawing on the floor.

At the doorway, you turn back to look at the room once more. The pentacle on the floor glows. You blink hard. The corners of the star light up as if candles have been lit.

"Uh, Dad?" you say quietly, tapping him on the shoulder.

When he turns back to you, the floor is dark again. You're sure you didn't imagine it, but will Dad believe you?

"Come on," Mom calls. "Don't fall too far behind."

You have to know if you imagined it.

"In a second," you tell Mom. You stare at the pentacle. Suddenly, you feel cold.

The star lights up again. Out of the corner of your eye, a shadow flickers. It exits through the door you came in from. You feel a strange pull to follow the shadow. But your mom is calling you again.

- To stick with the tour group, turn to page 52.
- To follow the shadow, turn to page 62.

You're not curious enough to follow that creepy shadow. You run to catch up with your parents.

Farah and Mat are leaning against a balcony railing. Farah sniffs the air. "You can't see it at night, but the ocean is just beyond those trees. In the daytime, patients and soldiers on the higher floors could see it and enjoy the beautiful view. You can smell the salty sea air from here."

The group walks past a set of stairs that has a rope tied across the front. A sign reads "Keep Out," warning of danger. As you pass by, you hear a sound coming from the stairwell. It sounds like your mom.

"Mom?" you call at the bottom of the stairs. The group has gone far enough that you can't tell if Mom is with them or not.

"Help me," you hear.

You're convinced it's Mom. And she needs you.

- To help Mom, turn to page 65.
- To get help from the guides, turn to page 69.

"I'll wait for my mom," you say, dabbing your bloody knees with your hand. "I'm sure she'll show up soon." The tour group must be somewhere nearby.

"Suit yourself," the nurse says. When you look up from wiping your knees again, she's gone. You hope she's gone to report your accident.

When the bleeding slows, you get to your feet and head for the stairs. Maybe it's best to wait for them on the ground floor. You begin the slow climb down.

Something moves along the wall. You turn to see a fleeting shadow.

"Hello?" you call out. "Mom? Dad? Mat? Farah?"

Instead of a reply, you hear a low moan. It sounds like someone in pain.

"Is anyone there?" you ask, swallowing the rising fear.

The moan grows louder. It sends shivers through you.

You take another step down the stairs and miss. You go tumbling down the entire flight and land at the bottom. Every bone in your body feels bruised. You try to call for help again, but you don't have the energy. You decide to wait for help. Eventually, you close your eyes.

When your eyes open again, your parents, the guides, and the rest of the tour group are staring down at you with concern.

"Oh, thank goodness," your mom says.

Your parents examine your injuries and put a bandage on your knee. Thankfully, you haven't been seriously injured.

You sit up, feeling embarrassed. Your parents help you into a waiting taxi, and you head to the hotel.

To this day, you can't be sure if you encountered anything paranormal. Perhaps it was just your imagination.

THE END

To follow another path, turn to page 11.
To learn more about haunted hospitals, turn to page 103.

The nurse insists that you follow her. You dare not say no.

You get to your feet and hobble after her. She stays way in front of you and doesn't turn back once to wait.

She leads you down one set of stairs and then through a long, dim corridor. Then she steps into an open area that's lit by moonlight. You blink twice and stare. The nurse looks slightly transparent. You squeeze your eyes shut and look again. Now she's gone.

You move a little more quickly. You don't know where the first aid room is, and you don't want to get lost.

Turn the page.

You walk as fast as you can past large open rooms with blue tiles. They're broken up by low walls. At the other end is another staircase, and you presume the nurse has gone this way.

In the corner of this area, you spot a door. It's ajar and you hope that you've found the first aid room.

You push the door open and find a small empty room. Where did that nurse go?

Something metal rattles. You follow the sound.

"Nurse? Please wait for me," you say.

You head to the next room. It has pink tiles on the floor. There by the far window is the nurse. She's holding a baby in her arms, rocking it gently.

"Where's the first aid area?" you ask, without thinking about where that baby came from.

The nurse says nothing. She continues to rock the baby. As you approach, the nurse and baby seem to fade in and out of the dim light.

Someone shouts something in a different language. It comes from behind you. The nurse turns. She looks terrified. She tightens her grip on the baby and runs away from you.

"Wait!" you call out. But she disappears—through a wall!

The shouts grow louder and angrier, and they're getting closer. You hobble faster away from them. You find a staircase and take the first step. You miss the next one and go tumbling down.

Turn the page.

You wake up to find that you're lying on a cot inside an ambulance. Your parents are squeezed in beside a paramedic who is tending to you.

"What happened?" you mumble. Your whole body aches.

Your parents look relieved to see you awake.

"You were found at the bottom of the stairs unconscious," the paramedic explains.

"We're heading to a hospital," Mom says.

You feel embarrassed to have been so much trouble. You can't quite explain how you got here. But you're glad you've left Old Changi. You decide that for the rest of this vacation, you'll stay away from anything scary.

THE END

To follow another path, turn to page 11.
To learn more about haunted hospitals, turn to page 103.

You can't resist the feeling that you have to follow the shadow. You run out the door you came in.

The shadow flies ahead of you. You pass many large rooms with low-walled partitions.

You follow the shadow to the balcony where it disappears into the night air. You stand there staring at nothing for a long time.

Something rustles the bushes down below. By the light of the moon, you can see only an overgrown garden there. You watch to see if anything moves.

Time passes and nothing happens. You yawn and stretch. Then you check the garden below once more before heading off to find your parents. But what you see freezes you in place.

There are people dressed in hospital gowns. They walk in neatly mowed paths or sit on stone benches. A few nurses offer medicines to their patients.

"What's going on?" you exclaim aloud. You look around, hoping your parents have come to find you.

When you look back down this time, all is still again. You can't explain what's just happened.

Turn the page.

This is too spooky. You run for the stairs and head out of the hospital. When you get outside, your parents are looking at you with curiosity.

"You were right behind us," Mom says. "How is it you've only just gotten here?"

You, Mom, and Dad are very puzzled. Time seems to have moved at different speeds for you.

You can't bear to think about what's really happened. You and your parents hop into the taxi and head back to the hotel. None of you speaks of this experience for a very long time.

THE END

To follow another path, turn to page 11.
To learn more about haunted hospitals, turn to page 103.

You hear Mom calling and you have to go, rules or no rules. You duck under the warning sign and head up the stairs. It's dark on this floor, so you shine your flashlight.

"Help!" Mom's voice echoes through the rooms. It comes from the middle room on the right.

The beam of your flashlight lands on a figure at the far end of the room. It takes a few seconds for your eyes to focus on who it is.

It's a young boy, not Mom. He looks about 7 years old. He's sitting on a stool and just staring into space.

"Hi!" you say, trying to sound friendly. "Do you need help?"

Turn the page.

The boy doesn't answer and doesn't move. You step in closer. "I'm here to help you," you say. He doesn't react. You try the phrase in Chinese too. He doesn't budge.

You follow his gaze to see what he's staring at. It's a spot on the side wall. It's unremarkable.

You get closer to the boy until he's about an arm's length away from you. You reach out to touch his shoulder and your hand goes right through him.

You freeze.

"Hey! What are you doing up here?" a voice says, shaking you out of your trance.

It's Mat. He stands at the doorway with his hands on his hips.

"Didn't you see the sign? This area is off-limits to visitors."

"I—I—uh—," you stammer. You can't find the words to explain what you've seen. "There's a boy..."

Mat grows thoughtful. "A young boy? Staring at nothing?"

You nod. Maybe you didn't imagine it?

Mat leads you back down the stairs. "There have been accounts of people coming across that boy," he says. "A lot of children came through this hospital over the years, so we don't know who he is. No one has been able to get proof of his spirit lingering here. You're lucky to have seen him. But you shouldn't break the rules here."

You feel bad and scared at the same time. "I'm sorry," you say. "So, you think I actually saw a ghost?"

Turn the page.

Mat shrugs. "Maybe," he says. "But I wouldn't repeat this to anyone on the tour. I don't want more people going through the barrier."

You walk in silence back to Farah and your parents. "Are you all right, Mom?" you ask. You still haven't shaken that terrifying feeling of Mom needing help.

"We're fine," Dad replies. "But you look a little pale. It's good the tour is just about over."

For years, you hold the secret of what you saw close to your heart. You feel special that you actually saw a ghost.

THE END

To follow another path, turn to page 11.
To learn more about haunted hospitals, turn to page 103.

You run to catch up with the group. They've made their way to the end of the hallway.

"My mom needs help," you call out. No one responds.

You walk through the group, searching for your parents. You don't see them. Looking at the group, you realize that everyone is standing still like statues. They're staring straight ahead. Their eyes are focused on Mat and Farah.

Mat is holding a camera to his face. Farah is frozen in place, her arm stretched out, pointing at a room. Her mouth is open as if she's speaking, but no words are coming out.

You grab her by the arm and shake. "Farah, I need help," you say.

Turn the page.

She doesn't move. You try that with some others in the group. Nothing.

You make your way through everyone in the group. It feels like a lot more than 17 people. Where's Dad? And Mom? Why can't you find them?

The hallway spins. Your eyesight blurs, and you can't focus. When you reach the last person in the group, you try shaking them too. They don't budge. Your head throbs, and your nose fills with the smell of bleach and disinfectant.

It overwhelms you. You squeeze your eyes shut. The next thing you know, you're on the floor.

You open your eyes and the whole group is staring down at you. Mom and Dad are kneeling by your side.

"What happened?" you ask, rubbing a sore spot on the back of your head.

"We were just listening to Farah talk about the wards when you collapsed," Dad says.

"Are you feeling hot?" Mom asks.

Farah brings you a bottle of water and encourages you to sip. "It takes a while to get used to the heat and humidity here. You'll feel better after a drink."

Mom and Dad decide that it's best if you leave the tour. You're disappointed, but you don't argue. This hospital is a strange place. You're glad you visited but you're also glad to leave.

THE END

To follow another path, turn to page 11.
To learn more about haunted hospitals, turn to page 103.

CHAPTER 4
TRANQUILLE SANATORIUM

You and your parents have been enjoying your vacation in Canada. Finally, the time has come for you to visit Tranquille Sanatorium. After arriving, you get out of the car and stretch. You gaze around the property. You take in the beautiful view of mountains and a large lake in the distance.

"Wow, I didn't realize how big this place was," you say. The three of you find the building where the ghost tour will begin. You all step in and wait quietly.

Turn the page.

Soon you hear a booming voice. "Hello! I'm Sue, and I'll be your guide. Welcome to our tour of Tranquille Sanatorium, one of the most haunted places in Canada," she says with a wide grin. "Let's start with some history."

Sue explains that Indigenous people first lived on the land here. They used it for fishing and hunting. When the British arrived, they brought diseases with them, including tuberculosis. In the 1800s, this illness killed many people.

"In 1907, this hospital opened to control the spread of disease. It began with 49 patients and grew to hold 360 beds. Eventually, an entire community grew in the surrounding area," Sue says. "Patients were able to work in the community as part of their therapy."

"The hospital has been closed for more than 40 years now," she continues. "Someone wanted to turn the property into a resort, but things didn't quite work out. For now, the building is abandoned. Some visitors like to explore it for signs of the paranormal. As you can imagine, with all the suffering that's happened here, there might be spirits lingering." She rubs her hands together as if anticipating something mysterious. "You never know what you might encounter. Are you ready?"

Some people in the group of about 20 visitors nod. You feel excited to get going.

Sue leads the group up a path bordered by large lawns. You pass several buildings that are two stories high. Some look like houses or apartments more than hospitals.

Turn the page.

A three-story building on the right catches your eye. There's a large mural painted on the side wall.

"That's one of the murals painted by the last owner," Sue explains. "This is a picture of his hometown in Italy."

You stand between both buildings. On the left is a two-story beige and pinkish structure with a greenish roof. The center has a triangular roof. The building looks old with several broken windows. It has two wings that spread out on each side.

"This side of the hospital housed the tuberculosis patients, including sick soldiers after World War I," Sue says as she gestures to the open front door. "The building on your right housed the patients with mental disabilities."

"I will be around in the hospital and on the grounds to answer any questions," Sue announces. "But we find that visitors like to pick and choose where to explore. If you end up on your own, we'll meet right back here in two hours. Please be respectful of the property and the spirits."

She hands out information leaflets, flashlights, and lamps. "You'll need these if you choose to explore the tunnels beneath the hospital. They're the spookiest part of this tour."

Your parents look to you. "Where would you like to explore first?" asks Dad.

- To explore the hospital building, turn to page 78.
- To explore the other building, turn to page 83.

You enter through the front door in the middle of the building. Narrow hallways with beige and blue walls greet you. You pick a direction and head that way with your parents following.

The hallway here is bright and you continue to walk past a lot of small rooms. There are tiles along the floor and walls in several of these rooms.

"There's so much graffiti on the walls," Mom comments.

"That's because these buildings were closed to the public for a few years," Dad says. "That's tempting for people to sneak in and leave their mark."

You find a staircase and head up to the next floor. It's a large open room, and it's a mess.

There are air conditioning vents running all along the ceiling. Many of them are ripped open at spots. The floor is covered with puddles of water. There are also broken pieces of furniture strewn everywhere.

As you tread carefully through the area, you find a few plaques nailed to the walls. They give some interesting facts about tuberculosis.

That's when you hear someone cough. "Very funny," you say. Tuberculosis patients would cough a lot. Dad must be teasing you.

Your parents look at you quizzically.

"Didn't you cough?" you ask, looking around. No other visitors are on this floor.

Mom and Dad shake their heads. They didn't hear anything either.

Turn the page.

As you continue to look around, you're sure you hear someone moaning.

"Mom, Dad, do you hear that?" you say.

Your parents hear nothing. They grow concerned about you. "Maybe we should check out the other wing," Mom suggests.

"Or I hear the tunnels are the highlight of this place," Dad adds.

You're shaken by the sounds that only you hear. But you also want to keep exploring.

- To visit the tunnels, go to page 81.
- To head to the other wing, turn to page 85.

"I want to see the tunnels," you insist.

In the basement, you see several walkways. There's debris on the floors, and you pick the path that's been cleared the most.

"There's another door here," you say, pulling it open to find yet another set of stairs. "Maybe this goes to the tunnels."

The stairwell is very dark. At the bottom of these stairs is a long, narrow corridor. There are pipes running along the wall on one side.

"Didn't Sue say they transported food through these?" you say, trying to keep the mood light. It's getting seriously spooky down here.

Turn the page.

"Yes, and laundry," Dad says, reading a leaflet by flashlight. "They used this to move dead bodies out of the hospital. They didn't want the patients to be exposed to dead bodies being moved out every day. It would've been too stressful."

You try not to imagine dead bodies being rolled down this hallway. But then the moaning begins.

"Dad? Mom?" you call out. Turning all the way around, you see that you're alone. Where did your parents go? You hear the clatter of something metal hitting the floor. It's coming from somewhere up ahead. That could be your parents, or not. You think about leaving the tunnels.

- To follow the sound, turn to page 88.
- To head upstairs, turn to page 91.

"Let's check out the other building," you tell your parents.

You walk across the lawn to the second building. You spend a few minutes admiring the mural on the side wall and bump into another visitor, a woman named Darlene. The four of you are the only ones who are visiting this building.

You look for the entrance. Darlene tells your parents that she's a psychic and has come to learn about the spirits that lived here.

Turn the page.

Dad holds the door open for you, Mom, and Darlene. The hallways in here are narrow. There are so many doors to so many small rooms. In its day, this hospital must have housed many patients.

Darlene scratches her chin as she chooses which hallway to walk down. She finally points to her left.

"Come on, this way," she says. "I feel strong spirit vibes in this direction."

Your parents hesitate and look to you. You're not sure you want to follow Darlene. You wonder if it might be better to explore with only your parents.

- To go your own way, turn to page 94.
- To follow Darlene, turn to page 98.

"Let's see the other wing," you tell your parents.

You head back downstairs and try to catch up with the rest of the group. You take the first step down and hear the cough again. You run downstairs and hurry across to the other wing.

The rooms here are similar to the first wing. There's a lot of damage to the walls and floors. But some windows on this side have white curtains that dance in the breeze. You pass a room with a bathtub in it. Another has an old toilet in one corner.

You come to a staircase.

"I wonder if the upstairs is one large area like the other side," Mom says.

Turn the page.

"Let's see," you say. If it's the same room up there, you'll get out fast, before the coughing begins. But you came here to explore, so you feel the need to at least check it out.

As you climb, you notice that everything feels heavier. Your legs slow, and your heart races.

You look at the room before you. You are at the other end of the same large room as you saw earlier. You almost expect to hear the coughing again.

But it's silent. The only unusual thing is the heaviness.

"I can't be here anymore," you say. It feels as if a dark curtain is falling over your mind.

As you stumble down the stairs, your parents grow alarmed. They say that you need fresh air. They help you out the front door and insist you sit down in the grass. After a few minutes of enjoying the sunshine, you feel better.

"We should go," Mom finally says.

You don't argue. Something about this hospital caused you to feel the way you did. You don't want to know why.

"Let's go home," you say.

THE END

To follow another path, turn to page 11.
To learn more about haunted hospitals, turn to page 103.

Your dad might have dropped or bumped into something, so you head toward the sound.

You follow the pipes on the wall until they stop. The hallway is wider here and there are small rooms on either side.

You don't see your parents. They don't answer when you call. The moaning grows louder. You search the first room but find it empty except for debris on the floor.

You shine your light. A pile of debris rises off the floor, twists like a mini tornado, and falls back down.

You step back out into the corridor. "That's not possible," you tell yourself.

You keep walking, looking for your parents. You check every room, but they're nowhere to be seen.

You reach the end of the hallway where there's a flight of stairs. Something behind you catches your eye. You shine your light on it. It's a floating blue ball. It's not attached to anything. You turn off your flashlight. The ball glows in the dark. You reach out to touch it, but it dodges out of the way.

"Okay!" you say. "I'll leave you alone!" You're totally freaked out now.

You hear Dad calling you from a distance. You run up the stairs. On the walls of the stairwell, you read the graffiti. "Help me!", "Get out now!", "Run!"

Turn the page.

You figure that's good advice and run as fast as you can until you're in the front hall.

Dad stands at the door. "We were looking for you everywhere!"

"We need to leave now," you insist.

Your parents don't argue. When you're at your car, you tell them about the floating blue ball.

"There have been reports of blue orbs floating in some rooms," Mom says. "Do you think that's what you saw? Orbs are said to be signs of ghosts."

You don't want to think about it. You just want to go home.

THE END

To follow another path, turn to page 11.
To learn more about haunted hospitals, turn to page 103.

You're not convinced that the sound came from your parents. If they've left you, then you're leaving too.

You hurry back the way you came. You don't remember the path being so long. You cannot find the staircase where you came in.

"Mom? Dad?" you call. Your voice echoes off the walls, but no answer comes.

Your heart pounds in your chest. You find it hard to breathe. Someone coughs and then moans again.

"Hello?" you say, flashing your light around you.

"Help," a weak voice pleads.

"Who's there?" you ask.

Turn the page.

Your hand shakes as you shine your light through the darkness. About halfway down the tunnel, a small blue light hovers in the air. You hold your breath.

The light grows in size. You realize it's coming toward you. You turn and run until you reach the stairs you came down. You take the steps two at a time, open the door at the top, and don't stop till you're outside.

"Where have you been?" Mom says. "You've been gone for ages."

You see that everyone in the group is gathered around Sue, who is thanking them for coming to visit. The tour is over. How did all that time pass?

You follow your parents to the car and refuse to think about what happened to you in the haunted hospital.

THE END

To follow another path, turn to page 11.
To learn more about haunted hospitals, turn to page 103.

Darlene doesn't seem offended when you refuse to go with her. You head the other way with your parents.

You walk down a long hallway. There are small rooms on each side. The ones facing the outside have a small window in each room. You walk into one of the inner rooms. There are no windows here. It's dark and smells damp. You can't imagine being a patient living here.

This room gives you chills, so you turn to leave. The room door slams shut. You rush forward and twist the doorknob. The door opens just a little and you push outward.

Suddenly, something on the other side pushes back. The door slams shut again, and you lose your balance.

"Help!" you call to your parents.

The door opens. Dad stands in the hallway, shining his flashlight at you.

"What was that?" he asks.

"Why did you stop me from opening the door?" you ask.

"I did no such thing," he says, puzzled. "We were down the hallway when we heard you call. The door opened easily."

"It felt like you were pushing against me," you protest.

Dad demonstrates by opening and closing the door again. "See? No difficulties here," he says. "Is this a joke?"

You don't understand. You know you didn't imagine the door being pushed against you. But you can't explain it.

Turn the page.

"Can we leave, please?" you say. You've had enough of this place.

Your parents agree. Soon you're back out in the sunshine, taking deep breaths. You're just happy to be outside. "No more haunted hospitals," you say.

You walk around the front of the building and see Darlene talking to Sue. The rest of the tour group mills about on the lawn.

Sue looks a little annoyed. "You're late," she says.

"It's only been a few minutes," you say. When you look at your watch, you realize you've been gone for two and a half hours. You're thirty minutes late!

You and your parents apologize profusely to Sue and the others. You cannot explain how this happened. Just as the group disperses and heads for the parking lot, Darlene pulls you aside.

"Time passes differently when you're caught up in the paranormal world," she says, abruptly turning away and walking off.

You shudder as you think of what she's said. Did you really disappear into the world of the dead? You can't wait to climb in the car and get as far away from here as you can.

THE END

To follow another path, turn to page 11.
To learn more about haunted hospitals, turn to page 103.

None of you want to be rude, so you follow Darlene.

The windows in each room are small, so they let a little light through. Some rooms are brighter because their windows are broken as if someone has thrown rocks through them.

You walk past several rooms without entering. Darlene stops at a few and simply sighs. She doesn't say much.

You read the graffiti on the walls out loud. It warns people to stay away.

You laugh, hiding your growing fear.

"Never mock other people's experience, my dear," Darlene says. "It may be a genuine warning."

Darlene stops at the doorway of a dark room.

"I feel a presence here," she says. "Do you feel the sadness in here?" She looks at you.

You look around. After a few seconds, you actually do get a growing feeling of sadness and desperation. It's uncomfortable and makes you want to leave. Still, you'd rather not tell Darlene about your feelings.

Darlene sighs and moves on with your parents. You linger a while, looking out the window to the grounds outside. You wonder who lived here. Were they unhappy? When you turn to leave, a girl is standing in front of you. She has long, black hair and is wearing a nightgown that goes to her knees.

"Who are you?" you ask.

The girl doesn't answer. You can't see her face. She floats away and stops at the door.

Turn the page.

Your whole body is shaking. This ghost reminds you of every horror movie you've ever seen. You want to run, but she's blocking your only exit.

There's only one thing to do—run right through her.

You take a deep breath, close your eyes, and run at her. If you can get past her, you'll head straight outside and scream for help.

Wham!

You run into something hard.

Oof!

That something falls backward with a yelp.

You open your eyes. You've run right into your dad!

You apologize over and over. You try to explain to him that you saw a ghost, but suddenly you feel uncertain. Did you imagine it all?

Luckily, neither of you is too badly hurt. You all go back to the hotel. For the rest of the vacation, no one talks about the haunted hospital.

THE END

To follow another path, turn to page 11.
To learn more about haunted hospitals, turn to page 103.

CHAPTER 5
HAUNTED HOSPITALS

Old hospitals can be great places for the imagination to run wild. Tragically, over the many years that they were treating patients, numerous people have died. Some died quickly, while others suffered long and painful deaths. Some people think that hospitals can be hot spots for the paranormal.

Some people take hauntings very seriously. They believe that spirits may have unfinished business on Earth. Some people think the ghosts may be lost and unable to find the path to whatever lies beyond death.

This is where ghost hunters come in. They seek out the paranormal and sometimes try to help the spirits move on. Some hunters report being hurt by ghosts. Others say they have been able to communicate with the spirits. They use equipment including EMF readers, sound recorders, thermometers, and advanced video cameras.

There are also skeptics who question if ghosts are real. These people point to scientific theories to explain some of these ghostly encounters. For example, an EMF reader going off could be caused by electrical currents in the area.

Yet not every ghostly experience can be explained away so easily. In this book, you've visited three of the scariest haunted hospitals in the world. Each place has a rich history. Stories of supernatural sightings at these hospitals have been told for years. Few, if any, have been proven true. What do you believe?

sound recorder

More Ghostly Encounters

There are many old, haunted hospitals in the world. Some of them were called asylums. They were institutes for people with mental disabilities. The old-fashioned methods of dealing with mental health issues meant that patients sometimes suffered terrible procedures.

The Athens Lunatic Asylum in Ohio is said to have a ghost of a woman who disappeared from the hospital in 1978. Her name was Margaret Schilling, and her body was found more than a month later. The outline of her body still stains the floor to this day. No cleaning can get rid of it.

Some visitors to the Trans-Allegheny Lunatic Asylum in West Virginia report hearing screams and loud banging sounds. Some have seen ghostly children wandering the halls.

Before doctors had the medicines to treat tuberculosis, hospitals would be full of patients dying from this disease. Some of their ghosts might still haunt these places. Other hospitals are said to be haunted by soldiers who died during wars.

Trans-Allegheny Lunatic Asylum

Other Paths to Explore

1. Imagine that you're a ghost hunter taking tourists on a visit to a haunted hospital. How would you prepare them for what they might encounter?

2. Imagine you're a student writing a paper about a haunted hospital in your area. Research a place and describe ghostly experiences you might expect to encounter there.

3. If you were a visitor to a haunted hospital and encountered an actual ghost, would you try to communicate with it? Why or why not?

Glossary

debris (duh-BREE)—the scattered pieces of something that has been broken or destroyed

disheveled (di-SHEV-uhld)—messy

musty (MUH-stee)—having dampness or a taste or smell of mold

orb (ORB)—a glowing ball of light that sometimes appears in photographs taken at reportedly haunted locations

paranormal (pair-uh-NOR-muhl)—having to do with an unexplained event that has no scientific explanation

pentacle (PEN-ti-kuhl)—figure of a five-pointed star with a circle around it often used as a magic symbol

skeptical (SKEP-ti-kuhl)—having doubt

supernatural (soo-pur-NACH-ur-uhl)—something that cannot be given an ordinary explanation

tuberculosis (tu-BUR-kyoo-low-sis)—a lung disease that causes fever, coughing, and difficulty breathing

Select Bibliography

Balfour, Seth. *Haunted Asylums: Chilling Cases of Deserted Psych Wards, Haunted Asylums, Spooky Graveyards and True Ghost Stories.* Published by the author, 2016.

Belanger, Jeff. *The World's Most Haunted Places: From the Secret Files of Ghostvillage.com.* Pompton Plains, NJ: New Page Books, 2011.

Colfax Haunted Hospital
colfaxhauntedhospital.com

Colfax's 'haunted' St. Ignatius Hospital featured on Travel Channel show
krem.com/video/news/weird/colfaxs-haunted-st-ignatius-hospital-featured-on-travel-channel-show/293-badcbed5-db31-4363-81f5-c9e4fea406eb

Ghostly Activities, "Ghost Hunt in Colfax, WA: St. Ignatius Hospital 4th & 5th Floor Tour," YouTube, June 30, 2021, https://www.youtube.com/watch?v=GD_Af2SYYvY

Haunted St. Ignatius Hospital
hauntedrooms.com/washington/haunted-places/st-ignatius-hospital-colfax

Lovejoy, Bess. *Northwest Know-How: Haunts.* Seattle: Sasquatch Books, 2022.

Read More

Atwood, Megan, Michael Dahl, Benjamin Harper, and Laurie S. Sutton. *Paranormal Stories to Scare Your Socks Off!* North Mankato, MN: Capstone, 2025.

Peterson, Megan Cooley. *Can You Escape a Haunted Hotel?: An Interactive Paranormal Adventure.* North Mankato, MN: Capstone, 2025.

Troupe, Thomas Kingsley. *Haunted Hospitals and Asylums.* New York: Crabtree Publishing Company, 2022.

Internet Sites

National Library Board Singapore: Old Changi Hospital
nlb.gov.sg/main/article-detail?cmsuuid=56d82afd-5b30-4e3a-8573-e3384797cd97

St. Ignatius Hospital
spokanehistorical.org/items/show/598

Travel Channel: 5 of America's Most Haunted Hospitals
travelchannel.com/interests/haunted/articles/5-of-americas-most-haunted-hospitals

About the Author

Ailynn Collins has written many books for children, from stories about aliens and monsters, to books about science, space, and the future. These are her favorite subjects. She lives outside Seattle with her family and five dogs. When she's not writing, she enjoys participating in dog shows and dog sports.